Learn How To Make Your Baby Smarter

By Margaret C Henry

Content

Introduction

You love your baby, of course. Nonetheless, do you love him enough to do whatever you can so he can realize his full potential and become a smarter baby?

You have a responsibility to help make your baby as smart and as capably equipped as it's humanly possible. If you want to give your baby a bright future, you should begin laying down the groundwork now. Making your baby smarter does not start when he begins to talk or when he starts formal schooling, it starts now.

The Early Stages Are Crucial

Brain development occurs in stages, which starts right in your womb. At this point, you have not much control over your baby's development. You can, of course, help the development along with eating a balanced diet, going for regular check ups and taking supplements made especially for pregnant women. However, you have more control over your baby's development once he is born. Then you should do everything you can to help make your baby smarter.

The first few years of your baby's life are the most crucial stage of your child's development. It is at this early stage that growth and development occur at a rapid rate; your baby's brimming with curiosity and eager to learn. Thus, you should do everything you can to help him along. Once a stage of development is done, you can't go back and play catch up.

Of course, your baby will develop without outside intervention. However, your baby would realize his full development potential only if you do give him external help.

Proper Nutrition

Proper nutrition is essential. In line with this, the adage "breast milk is still best for babies" reigns supreme. It is true and has been proven true. There are nutrients in the mother's milk that cannot be found in milk formulas. Moreover, breastfeeding is not only good for a baby's optimal physical growth; it also facilitates bonding between mother and child. Studies have shown that children who were breastfed tend to have higher IQ than children who were bottle-fed prematurely.

You can also give your baby vitamins that his pediatrician recommends to further ensure that your baby is getting the right nutrients at adequate levels. Aside from breastfeeding and supplementation though, there's one other thing that you should never neglect doing: provide your baby interaction and stimulation.

Interaction and Stimulation

You must interact and communicate with your baby. A baby is like a sponge and he would absorb everything readily and very rapidly, so if you want your baby to be smart, you must give him something to "absorb."

Make eye contact with him. Talk to him, too, even if he does not understand you. You should talk as if you expect a response. You must ask him questions and leave gaps so he can respond – this he will soon learn to do by cooing and gurgling.

Maintaining eye contact with your baby will help him assimilate your facial features and expressions. Conversing with him will help him recognize your speech patterns and tone. Soon, he will learn to recognize the various nuances in facial expressions and speech and mimic them. Both – eye contact and conversations – help build your baby's memory.

You must also hold your baby with apparent caring and affection. Your baby can sense when he or she is loved or merely tolerated. When he cries or give signals of distress and other ill-feeling, you must immediately respond. This early, you can have a great impact on your baby's sense of self-worth – and the more confident he is that he is loved, the more responsive he will be to you and to his environment and thus, the smarter he will become.

A smart baby also has a sense of humor. You can enhance this by tickling the baby. This can elicit giggling and laughter from and, at the same time, train your baby to expect things – light feathery touches lead' to ticklish sensation which laughter helps relieve – which, again, help your baby become smarter.

It's no difficult task to make a baby smarter. All you'll need to invest is your time. If you love your baby, you could surely give him your time? You are the real key to a smarter baby.

Part 1: Family influence

Chapter 1: 5 ways that bonding will make your baby smarter

Bonding is one of the first things your baby will enjoy when she is first born. As soon as you take her in your arms she will instinctively snuggle up to you and often take her first small feed from you. She will feel the comforting sound of your heart, which she has grown familiar with in your womb and the sounds of your breathing etc. All the familiar sounds of your body will be comforting to her in this strange bright new world. This is when a baby gets her first taste of bonding.

As the days go by she will be feeding and cuddling up to you. She will get used to your voice and gradually as her eyes focus will familiarize herself with your face. This bonding with her mother is one of the most important stimuli that she will have.

Bonding will make your baby smarter in a number of ways here are 5:

1. The senses of touch and smell are awakened: as you hold your baby close she will feel your gentle caress and feel the sensations of your touch. These stimuli at an early age will help to develop the senses of touch and smell.

2. Sense of recognition and association are stimulated: learns to recognize and

associate you with the basic necessities of life, nursing, comforting, etc. Your baby's memory will develop better as association is one of the keys to remembering things and events.

3. Starts to feel the emotion of pleasure and security with you: As she cuddles up to you, your baby will start to understand the positive emotional feelings associated with you.

4. Breast-feeding: The unique bond of mother and baby are greatly enhanced by breast-feeding. This has been proven to be a great stimulus to a baby's intelligence. Whether you choose to breastfeed or bottle-feed your baby, you should always remember the importance

of bonding. Feeding time is a great time to talk or sing to the baby while you cuddle him close to you. Maintaining eye contact with your baby while you feed him is also important. This can communicate to the child that he is safe and secure in your arms – and this will increase the bond between you.

5. Interaction: a baby learns to interact with you and understand the meaning of relationships. This will help her develop relationships in later life.

When you bond with your baby you will be stimulating many of her senses and laying the foundation for a smarter baby. This is a bond that will often last throughout your lives and is one of the most important relationships of your baby's life.

Chapter 2: The Power of the Mother in Making Her Baby Smarter – Learn by Example

The mother has a strong impact on how her baby turns out to be. A mother and a child share a strong bond that sometimes go beyond scientific explanation. Thus, if you want a smarter baby, the key to making this happen lies in your hand. Specifically, you –

the mother – are the key to making your baby smarter.

Babies Learn from Example

What the baby sees from his mother, he learns. This is actually good news. If babies learn by your example, then you will not find it hard to teach your baby. If you want to teach your child how to smile, he will do so if you demonstrate it to him. If you want your baby to laugh, he can easily do so by following your example.

The fact that babies learn from example, however, is bad news for parents who were unaware of that fact. In such cases, the mother might have been teaching her baby something she didn't want him to learn.

An Illustration of Learning by Example Gone Awry

For instance, some babies would amaze you with their definite preference for the television. Try as the mother does to get the child interested on a story or picture book, the child soon loses interest. However, when the television is turned on and played, the baby stares unblinkingly at the television set and never lets his attention wander from it.

Such an attitude would have been fostered by a mother who has the TV always on when caring for her baby. The baby would have been observing the mother's expression when she was watching the television. From his mother's reactions, the baby would learn to associate television with entertainment. He will soon absorb the same attitude and exhibit the same preference as his mother's.

While the television is not bad *per se*, the baby may become limited when he immediately learns to prefer it over other media. Due to his preference for the television, he may refuse to explore other avenues of learning such as reading books, drawing and coloring, or listening to music.

Maximizing a Mother's Power

The mother must be constantly mindful of what her actions are relaying to her baby. A baby does not only memorize his mother's facial features, her shape and her characteristics. He is also learning how to react and interact from his mother.   He is also learning acceptable attitudes and behavior from her.

Thus, if you want your baby to become smarter, then you should learn to filter your actions to show most of the positive things, attitude and behavior that you wish your baby to learn. Be happy when you are – smile and laugh a lot so your baby will learn them from you. Read books to your baby so that he will learn to appreciate the written word. You can also watch television with your baby, but make sure to tune in to child-friendly channels and to limit the time you spend watching.

You can also teach your baby about cause and effect through example. For example, before turning off the lights, tell your baby that you are going to turn off the light. When you have your baby's attention, flip the switch and be sure that your baby saw your hand movement. This will help your child understand that flipping the switch on the wall reduces the light in the room.

A lot of things can be taught your baby through example. You will teach him how to walk by example. You will teach him how to talk by example. This will make your job of helping your baby develop easier. Just be careful about the things you may not want your baby to learn yet which you are still unwittingly teaching him by example.

Chapter 3: Siblings – How They Can Make Your Baby Smarter

Your baby's physical and mental development is very important. Although it may sound easy, enhancing his mental development is not a simple task. Providing love and affection boosts his emotional quotient. Play can develop his balance and coordination. But making your baby smarter is quite different. There are many self-help books that can guide you and provide tips. Unfortunately some of these can be expensive.

Having many children can be rewarding and the same time stressful. Caring for your baby and dividing your time between your baby and the bay's siblings can be difficult. Fortunately there is a solution that will work for both of your problems, hitting two birds with one stone, so to speak.

Your baby can learn from simply interacting with you and her siblings. In fact your other children can help you take care and look after the baby as well as enhance your baby's development. Before you attempt making your baby's siblings help, though, you should ensure that there's no sibling rivalry that can impede your baby's progress.

Eliminating Sibling Library

The most common problem in introducing a new family member is sibling rivalry. Your other children may clamor for your attention and may become jealous of the baby.

One of the best ways of countering sibling rivalry is telling your children in advance that they will soon have a baby brother or sister. Before the baby is born it is important for the parents to explain about the baby inside their mother's womb. Take them when shopping for your baby's items and talk about sharing activities with their soon-to-be-born brother or sister.

When the baby is born your children will not have problems adjusting and will fully understand that the baby needs them too. The fact that you made your elder children feel that they were part of the decision to have a new addition to your family will also make your baby's siblings proprietary and protective rather than envious or jealous.

How Siblings Can Help Make Your Baby Smarter

Your baby's siblings are invaluable when it comes to helping your baby develop. Siblings provide a point of reference when the baby grows old enough to become aware of the difference between himself and other people. Your other children also widen your baby's horizon and expose him to more stimuli than what you can provide alone. having more faces to memorize and more speech patterns to remember have a positive impact on a baby's cognitive progress.

Your baby's siblings can also help a lot when you and your baby are engaged in fun, learning activities. Playing "Follow the Leader" or going around the obstacle course is more fun when there are more children following commands. With so many people to imitate or learn from, your baby will find it easier to assimilate what you're teaching him.

Making Siblings Help

Encourage your children to join in the fun when you're playing with the baby. Suggest the game peek-a-boo or hide and seek.

These activities are play for your older children so they're sure to enjoy them. More importantly, your baby is going to learn from them.

Let your baby's siblings build their own playground or obstacle course. This will not just improve your baby's motor skills but also encourage problem-solving skills as she goes through a maze of pillows, boxes and cushions.

If your baby has a big brother or sister, encourage him or her to read books or show colored pictures to the baby. Zoo books can encourage your baby to become familiarized with animals.

The moments that your baby shares with his elder siblings will not just encourage his growth and development. It will also make him feel better loved and strengthen his sense of belonging. Your baby will become confident and brave to explore on his own and learn on his own – secure in the knowledge that he is not truly alone.

Chapter 4: Environment: The Good, the Bad and the Ugly

How Your Baby's Intelligence Can Be Made or Broken by the Home Environment

Learning starts at home. It is the responsibility of the parents to teach their child the basics of education even before he goes to school. It does not only nurture the child's intelligence but also foster care. This will also give the parents the opportunity to bond with their children. Intelligence, by the way, does not only refer to a child's intelligence quotient; it encompasses emotional intelligence as well.

There are many ways to improve a child's intelligence. With enough patience you can improve your child's memory and cognitive skills. Apart from toys and educational books there are other factors to consider. To make sure that your child is both physically and mentally healthy, surround him with a positive and loving environment. This will prepare him for the challenges that he will encounter later in life.

The environment can have a profound effect on a child. His mental, emotional, and psychological development can be affected by his surroundings. During the early years the child is like a sponge, absorbing everything around him. Unfortunately, there are conflicts inside the home that can affect his behavior and development as an adult.

Effects of Divorce

There has been a high incidence of divorce and family dissolution today. Its effects are always experienced by the children who are sometimes forced to choose between their parents. More often they don't understand why their parents have to separate, and they are left confused and lost.

Children who come from broken families usually develop anti social behavior. More often than not, they come away from the experience feeling gloomy and depressed. Worse, they can even possibly blame themselves. They suppress their anger and have problems at school. Their behavior can range from mild to destructive.

A baby is not exempt from the bad effects of divorce or conflicts between his mother and father. Babies are extremely sensitive to the emotions that people close to them are feeling. Being surrounded by gloomy and depressed siblings and an angry parent or parents can have a negative effect on a baby. He may withdraw upon himself – become passive and not at all interactive or participative. This has negative implications on the baby's development. Only when a baby joins in on activities and accepts stimuli will he learn. Otherwise, he will stagnate.

Effects of Status of Income

It is understood that most children are not born with a silver spoon in their mouth. Love and affection is not just enough to support the growth of your child. Shelter, food and clothing are also important.

A smart baby is one who's healthy – and a healthy baby needs adequate food, clothing and most importantly a clean environment. Malnutrition can easily impede the growth and development of a child. It also makes him more vulnerable to diseases. Child mortality is often caused by diseases which are in turn, caused by inadequate nutrition.

The Ideal Environment for a Baby's Development

Yours need not be a perfect family or the biggest house in the block just so your baby would become smart or intelligent. The ideal environment where a smart baby would flourish without any difficulty is one where he feels loved and secure – an environment where people respond to the baby's cues and signals and where people hold, interact with and communicate with the baby in a positive way. It is also an environment where he is nourished physically – clothed, fed and protected from harm.

Part 2: Activity learning

Chapter 5: 5 strategies for making your baby smarter using fun activities

Playing with your baby is essential. You may not know it, but the interactions and activities that you share together can improve your baby's cognitive and physical skills. The time that you share together doesn't just promote bonding but can also enhance his intelligence as well.

Yes, pre-school can teach him the alphabet, but you can prepare him beforehand and boost his cognitive skills now. Playing with him can be exhausting after you have spent all night awake, and babies can be easily distracted. However, these should not stop you from trying to teach your baby valuable and necessary skills.

There are fun activities that will keep both of you interested. Consider such games your time to relax and your baby's time to have fun and to learn.

1. Wall Chart or Play Mat

Post a wall chart at his eye level. You should have a wall chart for numbers and another one for letters. The figures and illustrations on both wall charts should be large, vividly colored and easily discernible so that your baby will find them easier to grasp.

Bring your baby near to the chart and begin pointing out each letter or number to him.

Trace each character with your finger and encourage your baby to do the same. For every character you point out recite the name of the number or letter. For letters, you can actually give tangible examples (say A is for Apples and show him an apple if you have one handy).

Alternatively, you can use a play mat with letters or numbers so your baby can crawl along its surface and familiarize himself with the characters.

One word of caution, though, do not force your baby to respond or to remember what you have taught him. Learning and memorization takes time. Your goal every time you 'teach' him his letters and numbers is just to familiarize him with the shapes and figures of such numbers and letters – not to immediately understand what these signify.

2. Sing and Sign Songs

Learn hand signs for letters and numbers. While you sing the alphabet, make a hand sign in front of him. Soon he will be curious at your hand movements and imitate them. Aside from rousing his interest though you're your hand signs will also let your child learn and become more familiar with the sequence of letters and numbers. For instance, he will learn that the sign with the index finger extended from a closed fist means "one" and is followed by the sign for the index finger and ring fingers extended from a closed fist, which is a sign that means "two."

3. Roll a ball:

There are lots of other fun activities that you can do with your baby to stimulate his senses. You can simply roll a ball around and get your baby to chase it and return it to you.

4. Find an object:

You can simply go around the room, wait for something to catch your baby's interest, get close to that object or have your baby hold it when possible, and tell him the name of the item, its color, its size, its texture, and other such characteristics.

These activities provide a means for your child to learn about his surroundings and foster an environment where he is encouraged to explore, be curious and learn. In other words, these types of activities are the sort that can help you make your baby smarter.

5. Singing songs and music:

Sing to him the alphabet or numbers while you play. Soft and soothing music can be stimulating to the baby's sense of hearing and help him concentrate on the sounds he's hearing. You can also sing his books to him.

These are but 5 strategies through fun activities that you can enjoy with your baby and stimulate his intelligence.

Chapter 6: Speech and Communication

It is through the parents that the baby will first understand the world and what goes on in his environment. Specifically, he learns all this through his communication with his parents. Although the baby can only produce some unintelligible sounds, he is already talking with his parents and, in a way, telling them about what he wants and needs. Thus, it is important for the parents to respond to the baby's attempt at communication as this will increase the bond between the baby and the parents and, ultimately, between the baby and other people.

It's Your Voice that Counts

The advancement of technology has had an effect on the speech and communication development of the baby. Gone are the days when a mother usually just sits down on a rocker and talks or sings to her baby. Now, a mother can easily carry the baby around and sway her arms gently to the tune of the music in the TV or radio.

What she does not realize is that the baby does not need to hear sound, *per se*. He needs to hear his mother's voice. Letting the baby hear the mother's voice is very important as this allows the baby to focus only on one thing. When this stimulus is removed, the baby hears a lot of noise. This makes it harder for him to concentrate on and learn from one thing at a time. All these noises can also impede the baby's recognition of tone and speech patterns, and this can delay language development.

Your baby needs your one-on-one talks; these facilitate your baby's language and speech development. By learning what each sound means, what a particular tone signifies, how thoughts are expressed, and how words are pronounced and said, your baby will be able to absorb things much quicker – and he will become smarter because of it. Here are some tips on how you can make your baby smarter by communicating with him.

Tips on Communicating with Your Baby

When your baby is eight months old, he can now produce some "ba" and "da" sounds. You can strengthen this development by repeating such sounds and, at the same time, by introducing new yet simple sounds. Through this, the baby's speech will begin to develop as he recognizes more sounds and tones.

You can also encourage speech development not only by making him listen to the sounds you make but also by giving him something memorable to associate with such sounds. For instance, if you're introducing "da" or "daddy," you can point to his daddy – you can even let his daddy make the sound so eye contact between father and child can be maintained while the baby's being instructed about the sound "da" or "daddy" and what the sound means or refers to. This technique is even more effective as it includes as giving the baby something meaningful to associate with the sounds you're teaching him; this makes it easier for him to memorize and remember sounds.

You should also praise and encourage your baby whenever he produces new sounds that resemble an understandable word. This is positive reinforcement – it tells the baby that what he is doing is good and thereby encourages him to try producing even more sounds. Your encouragement will help a lot in your baby's speech and language development.

Communication is truly very important to babies. When you let your baby hear your voice, when you let him associate sounds with meaningful things, when you encourage his attempts at conversation, he will be able to develop his communication skills faster; thus, he will become smarter.

Chapter 7: Eye Contact

Eye contact is the best way to communicate with your child – and it is essential if you want to make your baby smarter. Making and maintaining eye contact with your baby facilitates memory building and thereby aids and abets the development of your baby's intelligence.

How Eye Contact Can Build Memory

We may think that babies cannot see during the first few days or weeks of their life, but studies have shown that they can. In fact, they can see whatever or whoever comes close enough (their range of vision is around 13 inches). Not only can babies see – they can even focus. When you're facing your baby, try slowly moving your face from left to right and back again. You will notice that your baby is trying (and succeeding) to follow your face's movement.

Initially, babies mostly see shapes and use them to identify people. As the days pass, though, their vision grows stronger and they can clearly see each facial feature and familiarize themselves with the people around them.

If you make it a point to maintain eye contact with your baby, he will respond and focus on you. This will help him get accustomed to you. He will begin to learn each feature of your face. He will learn to recognize you. He will study your facial expressions, too, and he will soon understand what each of your facial expressions signifies.

Maintaining eye contact with your baby therefore helps build your baby's memory. Soon, he'll be able to memorize things and other people's faces – and he'll learn and absorb more because of it.

How Eye Contact Can Build Intelligence

As soon as the baby can recognize and identify his mother's face, he can learn much from her facial expressions. This recognition of facial expressions can teach him about social interaction.

Say, for instance, you have just fed your baby. You gently pat his back and he burps. If this happens when you are looking at your baby directly, the baby will clearly see your reaction to his action. Based on your facial expression, he will know that what he has done was good. After being fed the next time, he will burp again; he knows that doing so is good and appropriate after feeding.

By looking him in the eye, your baby can see your facial expressions and learn from them. Thus, the baby will know how to respond appropriately to situations. This will help him greatly in trying to understand the world around him. In other words, this will help your baby become a lot more intelligent.

So the next time your baby is trying to make eye contact with you, look him straight in the eyes and talk to him. You can even make funny faces or tickle his toes to elicit his laughter.

Studies have shown that there is increased brain function and activity when babies are looking directly at the eyes of the person in front of them. This provides conclusive evidence that making eye contact helps develop the baby's brain. Eye contact is one key to building your baby's memory and making him a smarter baby.

Chapter 8: Mirror, Mirror on the Wall...

Why would you place your baby in front of a mirror and let him see his reflection? Contrary to what others may think, placing an infant in front of a mirror is not helping him develop his grooming habits – at least not in early babyhood. Babies do not yet understand what "handsome" and "beautiful" are. They can see plain features – eyes, nose, lips, face, ears, hair, etc. but they haven't yet learned the social judgment on what is handsome or beautiful. So, why exactly should a baby be allowed to see his reflection on the mirror?

Babies and Their Sense of Sight

In early babyhood, stimulation of sight can help greatly in the development of the baby's brain. Specifically, visual stimulation builds a baby's memory and therefore helps him learn about things. Visual stimulation, coupled with the parents' guidance and encouragement, helps the baby grow smarter.

When the baby is about six months of age, he gains a fully developed sense of sight. He can track things with his eyes and is already familiar with and recognizes the faces in his little world. He knows who his mother and father are and he knows who his siblings are as well.

At this point, the baby can also track with his eyes things that create sounds, say, a toy car that makes a honking sound. He follows it to whatever part of the room his parents place it. He also knows that that toy car is a fun thing to play with. Once he has it in his hands, his fingers would explore the different parts of the toy and he would even try to put it inside his mouth. This is also one of the stages where he develops his eye-hand coordination. For example, you put a toy in front of him and move it around. He immediately tracks it with his eyes and tries to grab hold of it.

Why the Mirror?

Knowing how important his sense of sight is, you should make sure to provide your baby with sight stimuli. Letting your baby stand in front of a mirror and look at his reflection provides just such a stimulus.

Initially, his reflection will just represent a new person to study and new features to analyze. His reflection will help him learn his facial features and his physical characteristics – even if he doesn't understand that it's himself he's studying and his own features he's memorizing. This facilitates the development of self-recognition and self-awareness. By letting him gaze at his mirrored reflection and by telling him that what he sees is his own reflection, you are helping him learn to distinguish between himself and other people and thus become aware of his individuality. Furthermore, by saying positive things about the reflection (praising the facial features of the reflection and giving him positive signals through your facial expressions and gestures) while the baby's looking at his reflection, you can help him form a positive self-image.

Fun Games that Stimulate Sight

Aside from letting him look at his own reflection, there are many games that the parents can play with their babies to stimulate sight. One of the best examples is the peek-a-boo. Babies love it when you cover your face and they'll scream in delight when you uncover your face and say "peek-a-boo!"

This game helps greatly in the development of his brain. He can learn that just because he cannot see you, it doesn't mean that you're gone. He will learn to anticipate the instances when you come out of hiding – and he will learn to appreciate your return. This is a valuable lesson since it teaches him that although an object seems to disappear, it will return sooner or later – and this gives him a sense of security and stability. You also get to share precious laughing moments with your baby so a deeper and stronger bond is created between the two of you.

Your baby's brain develops when it shows activity. Stimulating your baby's sight – giving him something to gaze at or giving him sight stimuli – elicits just such an activity in your baby's brain. Thus, if you let him study his reflection in the mirror and if you interest him with the things he sees, your baby's brain develops and your baby becomes smarter as a result.

Chapter 9: The Sense of Touch – How Touch Stimulates Intelligence

Touch has always been one of the special senses that are very important not only to babies but to adults, too. A touch has healing effects that can calm a person. The gentler the touch is, the more relaxed the recipient of the touch becomes. It is very important for parents to interact with their babies through the sense of touch because it is one of the most effective ways by which parents can tell their baby that he is safe, secure and loved by his family. When it comes to the development of intelligence, this special sense lends a big helping hand.

Intelligence and Touch

There is no doubt that the more a mother interacts with the baby through the sense of touch, the more the baby becomes aware of his surroundings. A baby can also feel and distinguish emotions just by this sense alone. For example, a gentle touch can calm and relax him while a rough touch can make him cry. In this way, the baby is learning how to recognize emotions and react to it, stimulating his intelligence.

This is also one way for the babies to explore their world. When he touches an object like cold water or soft stuffed toy, his brain is stimulated to understand if the object can hurt him or not. Through this stimulation, millions of brain cells are activated, and brain connections are made. The sense of touch then prepares the baby when it comes to shapes, textures, temperature, etc. although he does not know the significance of them yet. Through time, he will learn the difference between rough and soft textures, the difference between cold and hot and what can hurt him or not.

Tickling the baby's toes or tummy also stimulates his brain. This teaches him to anticipate things and respond appropriately. For example, you can play "this little piggy went to market" with your baby. Your touch and the sound of your voice will stimulate his brain, thus, allowing him to recognize different sounds and recognize body parts. He will also learn to anticipate that he'll feel very ticklish when your touch lights upon a particular body part, say his tummy. Thus, he will begin to squirm and laugh even before your fingers get there.

Implications of Lack of Touch

Today's inventions like baby strollers and little swings that rock them to sleep had robbed both babies and mothers alike the opportunity to bond. Remember, a mother's touch is important in the baby's emotional and mental development. Without this, the baby can grow up to be shy, withdrawn and aloof. Studies have shown that babies do die from the lack of loving touch. The negative effect of the lack of a loving touch is manifested in babies who have been left in orphanages.

Just because we live in modern times with modern inventions to help us rear our babies, this doesn't mean that we have to give up that basic, age-old knowledge that babies need a pat of affection and the loving touch of a human hand.

Chapter 10: Singing and music

5 tips to make your baby smarter

It does not matter if we have a good voice or not. What matters is that babies do appreciate our singing and the music we play for them. Studies have shown that babies do listen to music and to our singing. It has been proven that such stimulation aids in infant development. In other words, singing and music can make your baby smarter. Exactly what skills of your baby do your song and music positively affect?

1. Language Development

Sing in an audible voice: If you were going to sing to your baby, it would help if you sing in an audible voice and using clearly enunciated words. Minimize your baby talks – even if baby talk sounds cute, it is not going to help in the long run. If you sing with clear words, you are teaching the baby to recognize words and their correct sounds. Furthermore, make sure that the music you play – say, nursery rhymes – are calming to the baby. Again, choose records that have clearly enunciated words.

2. Movement Development

You can incorporate simple hand, feet and body movements that accord with the rhythm and beat of your singing or the music you're playing. This would help develop your baby's motor skills even more.

Babies do listen to us, so your singing and music can help the baby develop his gross motor functions. For example, the baby can learn how to track the sound of your singing. In time, he will learn how to follow the sound of your voice. This will help facilitate movement; he will look to his side or extend his neck to follow your voice. Music and singing can even facilitate rolling.

3. Object Recognition Development

Sing a song that contains objects, you can hold the objects in front of the baby while singing the words. This teaches them how to identify and recognize things. You can also let them listen to animal sounds then hold picture cards that contain the corresponding animal. Before long, they will be able to recognize animals and the sounds they make; they'll even begin to imitate such animal sounds.

4. Emotional and Social Development

Singing and music help babies emotionally and socially. When mothers sing to or play music for their babies, a deeper bond between mother and child is forged. This is especially true if the mother is holding the baby while she is singing or while the music is playing.

Singing and music also enhance the baby's social development. When he grows old enough to play with other toddlers, you will notice that he will sometimes communicate with other children by way of singsong voices.

5. Sing calm songs:

Most importantly, singing and music give babies a sense of safety and security. There is no doubt that lullabies can calm babies. There have been so many instances when children would ask their mothers to sing them a particular lullaby because it makes them feel better. What's surprising is the fact that the lullaby they ask for is one that they've heard way back when they were babies!

Indeed, the music you play for and the song you sing to your babies play a big part in his mental and emotional growth. You'd better start singing if you want a smarter baby.

Chapter 11: Taking Your Baby out – How This Will Sharpen Your Baby's Mind

There are a lot of activities that you can do with your baby. Unfortunately, with a pile of work on your desk and a mountain of laundry to do, time can be scarce.

Balancing motherhood and your career can be a feat, especially with a new addition to your family. However, your baby needs you now more than ever. Infants grow at a rapid rate so you have to pay attention. Apart from his physiological needs there are also other things that need to be provided. Occasional kisses and hugs are not enough, either. Time is what matters most.

Quality Time and Activities Matter

The moments that you share with your baby are very beneficial. Spending time with your baby strengthens your bond with each other. Apart from that, the activities that you share with your baby can boost his physical and cognitive skills. There are simple and fun activities that you can do to make him smarter.

You don't have to buy expensive toys or buy him a jungle gym. With the right environment and the right stimuli, your baby can learn to absorb things better and faster. These activities will prepare him for when he goes to school. They will also improve the development of his brain.

With fun activities he will also enjoy learning. This will be essential as he grows up. Going to school wouldn't be such a bore, this way. He will develop curiosity, and the interest in learning new things. Your influence can give him the head start that he needs.

Hanging out

It is believed that intellect is comprised of 50% genetics and 50% environment. With the right surroundings you can boost your child's mental development.

When you go shopping, you can take your baby with you. He will be stimulated by the different colors that he sees around him. He will also have the opportunity to hear new sounds and see new things. Talk to your baby while you walk and brose around the shops, and name the things that he points out.

According to studies, there is a relationship between the words your baby hears and his verbal intelligence quotient. This activity will also build his vocabulary.

Have picnics and let him explore his surroundings. Let him crawl on the grass, touch a flower or a tree. You can also go outside and play in the rain – just make sure that your baby is amply protected when you do so. Hop on puddles and relax on the wet grass. These will be fun learning activities that can help you teach your baby the difference between wet and dry.

There are a lot of things that you can show your baby outside your home. Sharpen your baby's mind by taking him out from time to time.

Chapter 12: The Power of the Printed Word – Books and Stories – Story Time

The growth and development of your child is very important. Every parent wants his child to be successful. To ensure this, parents can take advantage of the infant years to boost the baby's physical and mental development.

The period of infancy is the prime time for learning. Your baby doesn't have to learn the alphabet or the numbers at the youngest age possible. What's important is to enhance his cognitive skills for better brain development.

Do Not Force but Encourage

Parents often have this misconception that the earlier they teach their child to read, to speak, to walk, and to count, the better off the child will be. Children have stages of growth and development. They can not handle or learn something that is beyond their capacity. The goal here is not to make your baby a genius as soon as possible but give him the necessary tools so you can fully enhance and encourage his development at the particular stage he's in.

Your influence can give your baby a head start. Infants grow at a rapid rate, so you have to be attentive so you can cater to his rapidly changing needs. You don't have to buy fancy baby items or language CD's. There are simple ways through which you can make your baby's mind sharper. As long as the activities are fun and interesting, your baby will learn. When properly stimulated, babies can absorb more information.

The fun activities that you share together can be both rewarding for both you and your baby. As long as you keep the activities simple and fun, both of you will have a great time. The greatest tool that he can learn from is you. Your guidance will be a factor to his development which he will carry on later in adulthood.

Keeping It Simple with Books

Books are very good source of information. Choose books especially made for infants. Such books are full of colorful pictures that a baby will find extremely interesting and captivating. Make up stories that include the illustrations on the page. Better yet, read him books with fascinating stories. Such stories will give him something with which to relate the images. This way, your baby's imagination is cultivated and developed.

Other than pictures, you can show your baby letters and numbers. These are important because majority of the books that your baby will read as he grows up contain words and numbers. He doesn't have to learn the alphabet or numbers instantly. The goal here is to familiarize him with the figures that he sees. If he points one, simply name it. This will enhance his language and build his vocabulary.

Choose books that have one letter or one number per page and preferably an illustration to go along with it. This will make learning easier for him. It will also prevent the distraction or confusion that usually ensues when there are so many things going on. You can also sing him stories or make hand signs that relate to the letter or number on the page. He will soon try to imitate you. This will become his cues in learning sequences and this will also enhance his motor skills.

Books – especially picture and story books – are your powerful allies in developing your child's cognitive skills and encouraging the development of your baby's intelligence. Use these books' power well and you'll ensure your baby's maximal growth and progress.

Chapter 13: Hide and Seek – How a Small Game Can Have Big Results

A baby is primed for learning new things. Though there are boundaries to what he can learn at certain stages of his growth, you can still ensure optimal development by maximizing what he can learn at the stage of development he's currently in.

Fortunately for you, you don't have to engage in strenuous activities just so you can accomplish your goal of developing your child's potential to the fullest. You don't have to plot out an itinerary that takes your baby at a different place everyday, say, a museum today and a circus the next. Your baby can learn right inside your home. Just give him something fun to do. In fact, playing with your baby is already a step in the right direction.

Play with Your Baby

It is true that the more babies laugh, the more they learn. Babies can absorb better when properly stimulated. As long as the activity is interesting you will have your baby's attention. Both of you can share a fun, stress free activity that will enhance your baby's development.

Playing with your baby does not only serve recreational purposes. The games you play with your baby aid in your baby's physical and cognitive skills development. He will learn to associate reactions with actions. He will learn to move in accordance to the rules of the games. He will learn to memorize the appropriate moves and reactions. He will begin to copy the sounds he hears and the actions he sees.

Believe it or not, there are a lot of simple activities that can enhance your baby's development. Hide and seek is one. Peek-a-boo is another. Guessing games are fun, learning activities, too.

Hide and Seek

Hide and seek is a fun game that can boost your child's memory and help him better understand the objects around him. First, he will learn to memorize his environment. Second, he will begin to learn that where he sees you disappear is where he can expect to see you when you reappear. Third, he will begin to explore and move (thereby developing his motor skills) in his efforts to find you. Furthermore, if you prod him on with your voice while you're in hiding, you can enhance his ability to follow sound to its source.

You can modify this simple game of hide and seek to enhance your child's cognitive skills. For instance, instead of hiding out yourself, you can hide a familiar object and let him find it. By hiding something and letting him find it, you can help him understand object permanence. Object permanence is a term in psychology where a child understands that an object exists, even if he cannot actually see or touch it.

Peek-a-Boo

Peek-a-boo is another very simple yet extremely educational game that you can play with your child. Peek-a-boo is a fun game guaranteed to make your baby laugh so he's likely going to find it very interesting.

Studies have shown that surprise is an emotion that a baby is preconditioned to feel. What's good about this emotion is the fact that it actually prepares your child for another stimulus. Your "peek-a-boo" cry will surprise your baby and condition his brain to receive a new piece of information. When you appear, the visual stimulation that your sudden appearance brings actually increases brain activity. To make this game even more stimulating, you can show your baby a different colored or differently shaped toy every time you appear.

Guessing Games

Guessing games are also fun and educational. You can hide your baby's toy (it would be better if this toy is the sort that makes a sound) inside an opaque plastic container. Line this up with other similar containers and shuffle them. After that, let your baby guess or point to the container that has his toy.

This activity would enhance your baby's listening skills and help him understand the relationship between sound and location. This would also help him master tracking sound. This will also develop your baby's visual tracking skills when he tries to follow the progress of the container that holds his toy. Furthermore, this will help your baby understand that an object that is placed inside another object does not truly disappear; it is merely hidden from view.

There are a lot more games that you can play with your baby. Such games will serve their primary purpose and entertain your baby, but they will also help your baby learn a lot of things even as he plays.

Chapter 14: Feeding Time– an easy way to stimulate your child's intelligence

Learning doesn't have to stop during feeding time. On the contrary, feeding time can be a very good opportunity for stimulating your child's intelligence. All you need is a bit of creativity and patience.

Don't mind the mess

One thing that would help stimulate your child's creativity is allowing him enough freedom while eating. Children –especially babies – are messy. They just can't avoid staining their clothes or spilling some of their food.

While this may irritate you, remember to be patient. Go easy on your child especially if he is not even two years old yet. Freud's theory states that children develop their sense of neatness during the anal stage and that's when the child is 2 to 3 years of age. Thus, if your child is younger than that, be more lenient and be more accepting of the mess he makes. Laud the child's efforts to be neat when he eats and, if he fails to be neat, laud his efforts to eat. Allowing your child to explore while he eats will actually do a lot of good for him despite all the mess. It would help stimulate his creativity. Nagging him to be neat while he eats will only generate negative feelings.

Don't be conventional

Allow room for fun while your child eats. Try to change your routine once in a while. Replace his regular spoon and fork with fun ones like air-plane shaped utensils. This will increase the stimuli and also his appetite.

Another technique would be to clean some of his toys so that he can use them for eating. For example, a toy truck can be used to move some food around. This will not only stimulate your child's creativity but will also encourage him to eat more.

Play some games

Another way to enhance your child's intelligence is to play word games with him. When the child eats, enumerate the names of the foods he is eating. Say them out loud so that your child will become familiarized with them. Remember to exercise some variety while planning your meals so you don't say the same things over and over again.

You could also play role-playing games with your child. There are certain foods that can be used as props for role-playing. Animal crackers are perfect examples of these types of food. As you take one animal cracker, say the name of the animal out loud and proceed to imitate the sounds and the movements that the animal makes.

These games will help your child associate words with their meanings. In time, the child would grow up and learn to speak; encourage him to play the game with you.

There are a lot of other ways in which you can stimulate your child's mind while he eats. It doesn't have to involve expensive apparatus and toys. Just be creative and have fun.

Chapter 15: An Obstacle Course Game – an insider secret that not everybody thinks about

One important thing to remember when talking about your child's intelligence is the fact that intelligence comes in many forms or that it has various manifestations. People who are good in math or are good in writing aren't the only ones who are smart. There are actually eight types of intelligence. These are verbal-linguistic, musical-rhythmic, intrapersonal, logical-mathematic, naturalistic, interpersonal, and visual-spatial, and last but not the least, bodily-kinesthetic.

It is important to develop your baby's intelligence in all of these areas. Try not to focus on only one of them. Some parents tend to forget some of these intelligences, dismissing them as unimportant. When parents do this, children fail to become well-rounded individuals.

The bodily-kinesthetic aspect of intelligence is the most often overlooked in favor of other intelligences like logical-mathematic, musical-rhythmic, verbal-linguistic, and visual-spatial. However, this is an important aspect in a child's development – not only of his brain but also of his whole body.

Development

One good way to develop this intelligence is to create an obstacle course wherein the child could play. An obstacle course is a great way for your child to enhance many of his skills like crawling, walking, creeping, running, and jumping. This will certainly help give your child his much needed exercise thereby enhancing his bodily-kinesthetic intelligence. The various obstacles would also help to develop the child's problem solving abilities.

Assembly

Assembling an obstacle course is not hard. All it takes is a bit of resourcefulness and a bit of imagination. Instead of buying a ready-made obstacle course, you can use the things around your house. You can use a bunch of empty boxes as tunnels, a piece of rope for jumping over and for crawling under, and some of your chairs and tables to creep under.

Making Things More Interesting

The best way to make things more interesting is to create a story that goes along with the game. Tell your child that he's an explorer going through caves, cliffs, or rivers. Accompany your story with sound effects that would stimulate your baby's imagination. You could even join in the fun – you can make him go faster by acting as a monster that's chasing the 'hero' around. You could even place a doll at the end of the obstacle course and call it the 'princess'. Tell your child that his mission is to save the princess. Who knows, it might even foster his sense of chivalry.

You could also try switching the items around next time so that there would be a bit of variety when your child plays the game.

An obstacle course is indeed a great way in enhancing your child's intelligence. However, be sure to adjust the complexity of your obstacle course to the age of your baby. You should definitely not give your 8-month old baby an obstacle course meant for a two-year old toddler.

Chapter 16: Learning Toys – How to Choose the Safest and Best

Toys are not just for recreation; they can also provide your baby mental and physical stimulation, which can help them develop. The good news is that there are various toys for you to choose from. The bad news is that there are various toys for you to choose from.

Overwhelming Choices

The vast selection can be overwhelming. Even a single doll comes in a variety of brands, shapes, colors, and sizes. Furthermore, the lack of knowledge on which toy to choose for their child adds to the complexity of parents' task.

When you walk into a toy or department store, all the information you'd have are those printed on the box and the price tag. You will not see a guide that will instruct you if it is suitable for your child. The manufacturer can only suggest the age range of children who's capable of handling it. Perhaps the box will say that the toy is not appropriate for children below 3 years old because of moving parts which the child may choke on. However, most toys' literature is usually silent on the suitability or educational value of a toy.

Educational toys are easy to spot but choosing them can be stressful, too. There are not just many choices. They can also be more expensive. Some parents or grandparents surrender and choose what their children prefer. Others would buy toys that reflect their interest in hopes that their children will develop a skill. Fathers would buy their sons sport equipment in the hope that such sons will become interested in sports. Mothers will buy their daughters dolls so that she would learn to become feminine and gracious.

If you are toy shopping, you must remember that not every toy is suitable for every child. For instance, bows and arrows will be left unused; infants won't be able to handle them at an early age. A minute basketball set is sure to entertain your son, but it can definitely interest your daughter, too. Here are some factors to consider when you're toy hunting.

Factors to Consider

The most important factor to consider is safety. Make sure that it is safe for the child to play with, even when left alone. Infants are prone to choking; it is a part of their development to put everything in their mouths. Therefore, you should buy high-quality toys that are durable and has no detachable and moving parts.

Given a choice between a daintily made doll or figurine and a picture book, go for the latter and forgo the former. Your baby needs stimulation, yes, and both toys can provide him that. However, the first one will outlive its usefulness the moment your baby throws him clear across the room whereas the picture book will provide him many hours and days of learning yet.

The best kinds of toys always serve a purpose. They stimulate your baby's creativity and contribute to his learning needs. Choose toys that can improve his physical and cognitive skills. However, be sure to select only those toys that your baby can handle. Buy your baby toys that are appropriate for his age. For instance, educational toys like Legos and building blocks are wonderful for intelligence enhancement but they are hardly safe for your baby to play with.

What You Can Do

Play with your child as much as possible. This will serve three purposes. First, you will be able to keep track of his needs. You will also be able to recognize where his interests lie. Second, you will be able to monitor your baby's playtime and protect him from harm. Third, and most important of all, you can maximize the benefits your baby will get from his toys because you'll be there to provide structure and direction to your baby's playtime activities.

Chapter 17: Singing in the Rain: The Power of Water to Stimulate Intelligence

Water has always been an integral part of our lives. It sustains us. We truly cannot live without water. Just a few days without it would result to death by dehydration. It's such an important and useful commodity. But did you know that water also has the power to stimulate intelligence?

It's true. Studies show that babies who have been exposed to water, specifically water that they have "experienced" through swimming pools, have better concentration, social skills, and coordination. Furthermore, teaching your baby to swim and get comfortable in water early on might just help keep him safe.

Concentration

Water can increase a baby's concentration because as he learns to swim, he will have to concentrate hard so that he stays afloat and doesn't drown. Keeping himself afloat requires a lot of concentration especially if he's still at the process of learning this new skill.

Conceptualization

When you let your baby wade in the pool, you are enhancing more than his swimming skills. You are actually teaching him the difference between the sensation of wetness and dryness. In the pool, you can talk to your child and explain using clear and simple words that the sensation he's currently experiencing is the one we call "wet." After you get him out, dry him up with a towel and explain using clear and simple words that you are drying him up so he can be "dry" again.

Social Skills

Water can also increase your child's social skills. The pool is probably one of the first places where your child will get the opportunity to socialize with other people. The pool, specifically the public wading pool, is a place where other parents bring their babies and toddlers. Here, your baby can learn how to socialize or how to get along with his peers.

He gets to play with children his age. As he grows up, the pool will become a venue for socialization, and the acquaintances he meets there might gradually become his own circle of friends.

Coordination

Swimming requires a person to move his arms and legs at a certain pace in order to keep afloat. It requires a lot of coordination. With a bit of practice, the baby will learn how to swim and with this new skill, he will learn to coordinate his movements. His bodily-kinesthetic intelligence would therefore be enhanced.

Safety

Some believe that a baby learns how to swim even before he learns how to walk. They believe that this is because of the fact that the baby has been swimming in the water inside the womb (amniotic fluid) for a whole nine months.

While this may be true, it is important to keep in mind that accidents do happen. In order to prevent accidents, swim with your child. Keep him within arms reach at all times so that you'll be there to rescue him if ever something bad happens.

When the child is two years old, he might start fearing water. If this happens, do not force him to swim. Pushing him to do something he is afraid of doing might just leave deep emotional scars and his little fear might worsen and become a 'phobia'.

Teaching your child to swim at an early age helps, though. It's actually easier to teach a baby to swim than an older child. The earlier you start getting your child accustomed to water, the earlier your child can become comfortable in it.   This will help your baby enjoy the water more and thereby develop his motor skills and his intelligence.

Chapter 18: The Library – A Powerful Source of Stimuli and Fun

What is the first thing that comes into your mind when you hear the word, "library"? Was it the word, "book"? I thought so. After all, the library is technically a place that's packed full of books.

We all know and agree that books are very informative and are a great source of knowledge. However, today's children don't seem to think so. With the advent of television sets, computers and video games, children tend to wrinkle their noses at the very idea of 'reading'. And because the library is a place for 'reading', it's automatically labeled as boring or, in the words of today's teenagers, 'uncool'.

The Advantages of Reading

It is important to foster in your child a love for books and reading. Most substantial data are found on books; books are still the best source of accurate information. Also, reading is something that improves your child's verbal – linguistic intelligence. It improves the child's vocabulary, his grammar, and his creativity.

Though you may argue that the TV and the PC also help in that aspect, that doesn't change the fact that the child who spends 8 hours watching TV or sitting in front of the PC is more likely to have an eye defect than the child who spends 8 hours reading. Also, with books, you can be sure that your kid isn't watching mindless violence or lewd pornographic scenes.

With books, the child is forced to use his own mind to imagine or visualize and not just rely on the pictures on the screen to form an idea for him. This stimulates his creativity. When the child reads a book, he is immersed into a whole new world with limitless possibilities.

The Library

If you want your child to develop a love for reading, then it's best that you start early. Keeping books at home is not enough. You may have a lot of story books at home but it's still important to expose your child to a place with a wider scope, a place with more choices, and a place with lots and lots of books. That place is the library.

Some libraries have reading groups for toddlers. There is usually a 'storyteller' sitting in the middle of a group of children, animatedly reading a story for them. This storyteller can be anyone, from the local librarian to a parent-volunteer. A good thing about this is that it gives your child the opportunity to socialize with other children, thus improving his social skills or his interpersonal intelligence.

You can also visit a library where there are areas where parents and their babies can be comfortable and read story and illustrated books. You can both lie down on your tummy and let your baby turn the pages. You should simply describe in words the object in the illustration. If he's old enough, you can encourage him to repeat after you.

The library can be great fun for children. Given the right encouragement and the right activities in the library, perhaps you're children will find it even more fun than the adults that frequent it. Once your child gets used to thinking of the library as a fun place, he is more likely to want to return to the library and thus get all the benefits that going to the library entails.

Chapter 19: Chores as a Means of Learning

Sometimes, it's downright troublesome to get children to do their chores. They complain too much and when you finally get them to help, they do their job sloppily and messily. Sometimes it's just easier, not to mention faster, to do things by yourself. But the thing is, even if children may not really be 'helping' when it comes to chores, it's still beneficial to have them do the chores anyway.

Advantages of Doing Chores

Assigning chores to your children fosters a sense of responsibility. It gives your child a sense of belonging. Giving your child chores makes him feel important to your family. This helps build his self-esteem.

As the child grows, this sense of importance and belonging will be reinforced and strengthened and when he finally grows up, he will feel a need to be an active and contributing member of society, just as he was an active and contributing member of your family.

Doing chores also teaches your child about meeting expectations. However, remember that you shouldn't set your expectations too high or too low. Don't get mad at him when he doesn't meet your expectations – you are setting him up for frustration that way. However, don't just say 'at least you tried' because that would be setting your and your child's expectations too low.

Instead, focus on the task you're giving him. Make sure that it is something that he has the capacity to accomplish. Don't make it too hard or too easy. If he expresses difficulty, assist him in doing the chore. The important thing is to make sure that he accomplishes it. Then, once he accomplishes it, praise him for a job well done. This will enforce a positive behavior for chores and drive him to keep accomplishing them because of the affirmation he gets when he succeeds.

When to Start

You should start early when teaching your child to do chores. Remember that according to Erik Erikson's developmental theory, children in the preschool age are on the developmental task of "initiative vs. guilt". This is the time when they are trying to be 'important'. During this stage in his life, it is important to allow him to feel important.

Also, at this stage, you should start assigning him some easy tasks like putting his toys back into their proper places after he finishes with them. As he grows, progress to more difficult tasks that are more appropriate for his age and abilities.

Your months-old baby should also not be exempt from learning through chores. You can give him simple 'fetch chores.' For instance, you can ask your baby to fetch his ball from the corner of the room. After he does so, play with him using the ball he got for you.

Remember, your child may be slowing you down in your chores now but someday, you're going to be too old and too tired for all the chores and you're going to need all the help you can get. Your child might just be the one to help you then. More importantly, though, getting your child accustomed to chores now will help him grow to become a responsible and motivated individual.

Chapter 20: Rest and Explore

Giving birth to a modern-day Mozart or Einstein is the dream of most parents. In the hopes of realizing this dream, they tend to give their child truck-loads of stimuli, unaware that too much stimulation can do more harm than good. I'm not saying that it's bad to expose your child to stimuli. I'm just saying that you should not expose your child to too much of it because it won't do you or your child any good.

Why the Brain Needs Rest

People are exposed to millions of stimuli everyday. However, the brain cannot process all of these stimuli at once. The brain can only process a fraction of it. Thus, even if you play all of Mozart's songs in one day, chances are, your child would only be able to assimilate one or two of the songs.

Do you notice that when you are listening to a lecture and the lecturer speaks too quickly, you'll find the lecture more difficult to follow? That happens because your brain needs time to process the data you have already received. You need time to allow the new ideas to sink in so that you will have a full understanding of the topic. Well, the infant's brain more or less works the same way. You need to give his brain time to process the information or the stimuli supplied.

Thus, if you're playing some of Mozart's classics to your child, don't let it play for a whole 24 hours. Play a bunch of songs then let the child rest for a while. There's no need to overload him with sensations. Watch out for cues that tell you that your child is becoming over-stimulated. These cues range from blatant to subtle ones. Blatant cues include actions like crying, fussing, and restlessness. The subtle cues include inattentiveness and diverting his or her gaze whenever you try to show him or her something.

What to Do If Your Child Is Over-Stimulated

Be sensitive to your child's needs. As much as you want him to become the next Mozart, you will still have to cater to his needs and your Mozart-training will just have to wait. Remember that he has just recently been exposed to this world. If your child becomes over-stimulated, just take him to a quiet place and allow him to rest. It might also help if you wrap him in a blanket and tuck in his arms and legs. This helps because this simulates the setting of the womb where he has been so comfortable.

When your baby is done resting, you can assist him in exploring his new world again. Remember this pattern: Rest and Explore. If you do things right, you're sure to become closer to your goal of raising the next Mozart – and perhaps even the next Einstein.

www.ingramcontent.com/pod-product-compliance
Lightning Source LLC
Chambersburg PA
CBHW050803080726
47818CB00039B/419